Modern Publishing's Unauthorized Biography of

JOE
McINTYRE
of the
NEW KIDS ON THE BLOCK

By Gary Poole

D1277647

Modern Publishing
A Division of Unisystems, Inc.
New York, New York 10022

Book Design by Bob Feldgus

CONTENTS

Joseph Mulrey McIntyre—a.k.a. Joe, Joey Joe, Joe Bird, or Bird.
Chris Mackie

INTRODUCTION

Joe McIntyre, the Kid who has been called "the heart-throb of the group," is the youngest member of New Kids On The Block, the hottest group in show business today. He was the last to come on board, but he's certainly not the least. In fact, thousands of fans think he's the most!

Charming, friendly, and caring, this New Kid certainly knows what makes him happy, and at the top of his list is singing his heart out for his loving fans.

There are so many things about Joe that endear him to his fans that it's difficult to name them all. For example, he carries a teddy bear with him while on tour to fend off the feeling of homesickness. And success hasn't changed him one bit. He still considers the friends he grew up with back home to be his closest pals. Whatever Joe does is real and honest. He's simply a natural! That's one of the reasons he's got such a loyal following.

Before becoming a member of New Kids On The Block, Joe was just another average guy, a bit stage-struck (make that a lot!) with a beautiful singing voice and sweet good looks. Then lightning struck in the form of record producer Maurice Starr—and Joe's life hasn't been the same since! It's like being caught up in a whirlwind or tornado, lifted up and carried off to the Land of Oz. Only with Joe there are no wicked witches—just good friends in the form of Danny, Donnie, Jordan, and Jon!

It's magical and Joe loves every minute of it—the travel, the screaming, adoring fans, the music, and the joy of performing with guys who have become like brothers to him. It all combines to make Joe's life a dream come true.

Millions of record buyers yearn to see and hear more, and a lot more is coming in the form of more albums, singles, TV appearances, concerts, and yes, even a movie. What's more, parents like them, too! They're a far cry from the frenzied rockers and heavy metal screamers that turn parents off. The New Kids On The Block are decent and wholesome young men with solid values who literally could be almost anyone's neighborhood kids on the block.

And that's a key to their success. They're so amazingly popular with their fans, because they're so much like their fans!

In just a few years, Joe and the others have become veteran entertainers, performing before thousands of cheering fans. They've shared the stage with such famous musicians as Miami Sound Machine, the Pointer Sisters, and Tiffany. In fact, it was Tiffany who gave them their first big break when she let them be her opening act. Since then, their rise has been so swift, that now Tiffany has performed as *their* opening act!

Has their rise to super-stardom been too quick? Has it been too much, too soon? Joe and the others don't think so. They have sacrificed a good deal and worked extremely hard to get where they are, and deserve every bit of success they have.

So how is Joe taking all this? How is he able to keep his head? How does he relax? What are his hobbies? Does he have a steady girlfriend? In short, what is Joe McIntyre really like?

For the inside scoop, read on.

1

FAMILY TIES

How important is Joe's family to him? Well, Joe's family is his greatest treasure and ranks number one in his life. Without the love and support of his family, Joe wouldn't be where he is today. Of course, being a member of New Kids On The Block comes in a close second.

On December 31, 1972, at Glover Hospital in Needham, Massachusetts, a blue-eyed baby boy was born into the McIntyre family. Cute and cuddly even then (he hasn't changed much; he's *still* cute and cuddly), Joe became the newest and last member of the large McIntyre family. Joe has one brother, Tom, and seven sisters, Judith, Alice, Susan, Patricia, Carol, Jean, and Kate.

How did Joe get his name? His mom had already decided to name this baby Christopher, but at the last minute, Joe's dad decided that he would be named Joseph Mulrey after a close family friend.

Though Joe's mom always calls him Joseph, he is Joe to almost everyone else—unless he's called by one of his family nicknames. After all, what are nicknames if not terms of endearment? And this Kid, always doted on by his brother and sisters is very dear, indeed. Somehow, Joe's very cuteness seemed to demand a lot of nicknames so he found himself being called "Joey Joe," "Joe Bird," and sometimes just plain old "Bird."

The only time Joe ever minded having a nickname

Believe it or not, Joe has never had a formal singing lesson in his entire life. Todd Kaplan, Star File

was when he first joined New Kids On The Block, and the other Kids called him "Slow Joe" for not picking up a dance step immediately.

Joe's father, a bricklayer and vice president of the National Bricklayers' Union in Boston, always worked long hours. He can point with pride to many beautiful homes he helped to build in and around the Boston area. Joe's mom, Kay, worked as a secretary for the Greater Boston Boy Scouts—a job she took because it was near home and enabled her to keep tabs on her nine children.

With such a large and active family, it would have been easy for everyone to make different plans and go their own separate ways. But Mr. and Mrs. McIntyre made a point of insisting that everyone eat dinner together promptly at 5:30 each evening.

Joe's house, which was fairly large, was set atop a hill on a street not far from the neighborhood park and pond. It was a great place to grow up and Joe spent a lot of time playing in that park with his best friend who lived across the street.

Once some of Joe's older sisters started to move out, there was more room in the house, but Joe still shared "the little room" with his brother Tommy. They slept in bunk beds and covered their bedroom walls with sports posters. Like a lot of boys, Joe also had a collection of baseball caps from almost every team in the country!

Two other important items in Joe's room were a television set and a stereo. These had a profound influence on Joe, who used to spend hours listening to Michael Jackson records, and learning how to imitate him. Michael J. was (and still is) an idol of Joe's, although Frank Sinatra is his current favorite. Although Joe confesses to liking all types of top 40 music, back in elementary school, Joe's taste was much more limited. He was not into rapping or rhythm and blues music as were Donnie, Danny, Jon, and Jordan, who learned to rap and breakdance from their schoolmates at William Monroe Trotter, the elementary school they were bused to in Roxbury.

Joe attended kindergarten at Agassiz School near his house. After Agassiz, Joe attended another parochial school, St. Mary's of Assumption School in Brookline until he was ready for the ninth grade. At St. Mary's, Joe was taught by nuns and wore a school uniform. He made very good grades but lacked some discipline. It seems Joe just couldn't stop talking out of turn or getting out of his seat without permission.

Though surrounded by so many older siblings, Joe still found time to spend alone in his room drawing, sketching, and daydreaming about what he would like to do or be. Whether drawing, singing, or acting, Joe's parents always encouraged all of their children to develop their talents. Joe is grateful for his parents' support and positive attitude. "In our family, whatever one of us does is accepted by the others," he explains.

Performing, whether onstage at a neighborhood theater or in the church choir, has always played an important role in the McIntyre family. Joe's mom, always a performer at heart, set an example early in their lives by joining the local community theater group. She sang, danced, and acted in many local productions. No doubt this served as an example for Joe who was always extremely close with his mother.

Three of Joe's sisters also felt the lure of the stage. Carol and Susan were in some local productions, but sister Judith was the first to make a career in show business. She has appeared on television in *The Guiding Light* and *One Life to Live*. Joe is very proud of Judith and loves to announce her accomplishments. "My sister got rave reviews in the New York Times for her portrayal of Peg in the play *Peg Of My Heart,*" he says. "She's a terrific actress!"

Even Joe's dad got in a little acting experience. He once appeared in a television commercial for Massachusetts governor Michael Dukakis.

Joe has never had a formal singing lesson in his life, and says that he still doesn't really sing correctly. He joined the church choir at age six and simply began singing! At about the same age, he became involved in theater and added acting to his list of talents.

The choir director of St. Thomas Aquinas, the church Joe and his family attended regularly, founded the Neighborhood Children's Theater (NCT) of Boston, a fairly large theater group numbering approximately sixty or seventy youngsters. Joe, who was already singing in the church choir, joined NCT and performed in musical productions such as *Oliver!* and *The Music Man,* as well as dramatic plays including *Our Town.* The first time Joe performed onstage was when he was six years old and sang a duet with his

When Joe was just a little kid he used to pretend to be a rock star and now it's the real thing! Ernie Paniccioli

sister Carol. Joe still remembers how much he loved the applause!

Performing on weekends and holidays with the NCT

Joe joined the church choir at age six and has been performing, and loving the applause, ever since. Larry Busacca/Retna

proved to be a great training ground for Joe professionally. By now, he was fully bitten by the performing bug. Joe believes that those early years of performing really helped to prepare him for the New Kids.

Soon, Joe branched out and began performing with other community theater groups. He just absolutely loves to perform, and that's what comes across to audiences everywhere. And the fans love him right back!

With such a big family, there were a lot of fun times around the McIntyre house. The most fun were holidays, when the relatives descended upon the scene adding more joy and excitement to an already large and happy household.

"We'd perform for our relatives," recalls Joe. "My brother and me used to make believe we were playing guitars, pretending to be rock stars!" Little did he know that in a few short years that "pretending" would become a reality!

Christmas is still the favorite holiday for the McIntyres. Since three of his sisters now live in different cities, and Joe is on the road so much touring with the New Kids, Christmas is about the only time the entire McIntyre brood can get together.

And now, Joe can at long last afford to buy really neat presents for his brother and sisters, mom and dad. In fact, with his new-found success, he was able to buy his mother a mink coat that she'd always dreamed of owning.

Joe's closest friends remain those he grew up with. These are the ones he comes home to after a long haul on the road. He knows that they like him for himself, and not because he has become a superstar with New Kids On The Block.

That's one of the problems of being famous. It's difficult to know if the people he meets now like him as Joe, or because he's a celebrity. With his old friends, he doesn't have to worry. They knew him when he

13

really *was* just another kid on the block! Now, though, instead of doing homework or tossing a football around, it's more likely to be a game of golf or racquetball that they enjoy.

The fact that Joe hasn't turned his back on his old friends shows just what a regular guy he really is. He doesn't come on like a big shot or anything like that.

Judy McIntyre, Joe's oldest sister, confirms that Joe is still the same nice, sweet, generous, funny, cuddly kid he's always been, and that the only changes in him are the ones that come with maturity.

Joe was twelve years old when he joined New Kids On The Block. So that meant when he entered Catholic Memorial High School, he was already hard at work doing his bit to help launch New Kids on the road to stardom. They weren't an overnight success by any means. It took years of hard work before the New Kids hit it big with *Hangin' Tough.*

Joe realizes that he missed some important parts of growing up—not being able to attend high school with his friends or be involved in typical extra-curricular activities. And, of course, he has virtually no privacy. Touring with the New Kids brought an abrupt change to any sort of a "normal" life.

"It's not always fun," he says. "Sometimes I'd rather be home playing sports with my friends. But I really enjoy being with this band. I've become close friends with the other guys. I never mind not being able to chill out at home with my friends, because I can still chill out with Donnie, Danny, Jon, and Jordan."

SEARCHING FOR JOE

What's it like being the youngest member of New Kids? At first, it wasn't easy, that's for sure! Joe was brought in as a replacement for Jamie Kelly who was one of the original five. He left the group, so the story goes, because his parents simply didn't want him to be in show business. So that left a vacancy to be filled. To make matters even more difficult, Jamie was a good friend of Donnie's—one of his "homeboy" friends at that!

It's a tough job taking the place of someone else in *any* situation, but when that someone is already a good buddy of all the other members of the group, then it's even harder. So poor Joe had to be ten times better, just to prove himself equal to the former member! After all, he was replacing a friend of Donnie's, and the fact that Joe was only twelve years old didn't help much either.

When Joe came on board, he not only was two years younger than the youngest member (Jordan), he was a lot smaller than the others, too. In fact, when Joe joined the group, he was not even five feet tall and only weighed about ninety pounds, which made him even easier to pick on.

Instead of being the adored baby that he'd always been at home, with seven older sisters ready to fulfill his every need, Donnie, Danny, Jon, and Jordan just saw a scrawny little kid with a different background who was immediately being given the leads to sing.

Ironically, one of the very reasons Joe was picked to be in the group was because he *was* younger, sweeter looking, and different from the others. Record producer Maurice Starr definitely wanted the fifth Kid to be younger than the others—someone who easily

Though Joe says he's not really looking for a girlfriend, he would like to meet someone "cool, chill, and smart." Ernie Paniccioli

could hit the all-important high notes. Donnie, Danny, Jon, and Jordan were all clean-cut teenagers, but they had some rough edges. That's one of the things that makes them so appealing. But the group needed some sweetness, too. The contrast, Maurice reasoned, would be good. Foremost in Maurice's mind, of course, was his own memory of the young Donnie Osmond and Michael Jackson, both of whom started in show business when they were practically no more than toddlers!

Maurice laid out his plan to Donnie, Danny, Jon, and Jordan. He described the sweet, high-pitched voice he needed to round out the group. And he wanted a Kid who could become a teen idol as well. So that meant that the newest New Kid not only had to sing well, but be cute, too. Joe, by the way, is the last person in the world to think he's cute!

At any rate, the plan was clear to everyone, and the only problem was finding the as yet undiscovered Kid who could fill the bill!

Joe will never forget his audition day because it also was Father's Day—June 15, 1985. Joe knew that if he were successful in this audition, it would be a wonderful Father's Day present for his dad.

The thought of seeing his son catapulted into fame and fortune was something Joe's father had never even dreamed about, much less considered! Yet, there was his son, going off to try out for something that could very well change his entire life—and the lives of his entire family!

Mary Alford (formerly Maurice Starr's talent man-ager) picked Joe up in her car and ___ just

Maurice's house for the ___

songs the group was ___

Maurice and Ma___

car, Mary poppe___

be in the gr___

Joe is quite the impressionist, a talent he developed from imitating members of his family. Ernie Paniccioli

looked at her for a moment, not sure if all this was really happening. Then she said, "You've got the part!" Joe just sat back in his seat. All he could manage to say was, "Well, here I am!"

Perhaps, the fact that it was Father's Day had something to do with how good Joe's audition was. It may have given him the added enthusiasm that was needed to put him over the top. Joe's ties to his family are very strong, and that may have been in the back of his mind, spurring him on when he walked into that audition.

Boy, did he have enthusiasm! That, coupled with his talent and looks was an unbeatable combination! Starr was so impressed that he signed Joe up

ded the songs, and the rest is his-

BEING ACCEPTED

Interestingly, the McIntyre home is not very far from Dorchester or Roxbury where the other New Kids lived and went to school. However, Dorchester and Jamaica Plain where Joe lived were very different kinds of neighborhoods, and Joe never met Donnie, Danny, Jon, or Jordan until the fateful day when he became the fifth member of the New Kids On The Block.

"It was weird," says Jon. "I hate to say it, but we used to pick on Joe, give him a hard time."

"Most of us are from the streets," says Donnie. "Don't get me wrong, we weren't hoods or anything like that, but we were heavy into the streets, not the drug scene or anything. I was really into break dancing, so I was on the streets a lot!"

So sweet, innocent Joe seemed like a real square to them. Donnie was the toughest to get to know and picked on Joe the most. "I had trouble accepting him," Donnie admits. "He looked kind of square, and we weren't sure he was going to fit in."

Even though Donnie started off bullying Joe, soon he began to feel like an older brother to him. Instead of picking on Joe, Donnie wanted to help teach Joe things and set a good example for him. The more they got to know each other, the more they liked and respected each other.

"And you know what?" Donnie admits with a grin. "I look at Joe now, and I see a younger version of me. Yeah, Joe's a lot like me."

Perhaps, being so much alike is what made Donnie and Joe argue so much. "It's funny," says Joe, "but sometimes Donnie and I get on a roll and it's non-stop arguing. The rest of the time, we're fine. We're really good friends."

Jon says, "The thing about Joe was, he'd hold a grudge longer than any of us, but he gets over it, and we're back to clowning around and goofing on each other."

Piled on top of all that stress was homework! Joe still had the burden of a full schedule of classes. The fact that he was an honor roll student gave him even more pressure. In fact, when the group first took off, Joe had to work with a tutor while on the road, and to his dismay found that he did not make the honor roll for the first time in his high school career. But that soon changed, and he got back on the honor roll again.

After all he had to go through, it's a wonder Joe stuck with it at all. Lesser kids would have given up. Frequently, Joe would go home crying after rehearsals, but Mary Alford, as well as Joe's family, encouraged him to stick it out. Joe's inner strength and determination, the encouragement he got, and the simple fact that he loves to perform kept him going.

So, you see, Joe was hangin' tough before the album *Hangin' Tough*. Soon the other Kids began to respect Joe, not only for his talent, but for the great guy that he is. And it was then that the New Kids On The Block began to feel like a family! Suddenly, Joe had two families—his own and the group!

Now the confidence and support they give each other is one of the more important reasons for the group's success! Before each performance the New Kids go into a huddle, and pump each other up so when they hit that stage, they're ready to rock!

Looking back now, it's hard for them to remember when they weren't like a family. Fans can see they're a bunch of nice guys who really like each other, like what they're doing, and who really love their fans! More than anything else, they all want to put on a good show.

Joe has just graduated from Catholic Memorial High School. Though college has been postponed, Joe is thinking about taking some college courses in music and English. Whatever his plans for the future, Joe plans to stay with the New Kids a long, long time.

Joe fulfilled Maurice Starr's vision for the group—a younger boy with an adorable face and sweet voice who could hit the high notes.
Chris Mackie

Getting ready for a show requires a sound check, interviews with the press, and drinking a soothing blend of honey and lemon tea.
Janet Macoska

PART 2

BEING A STAR

What's it like being a part of the musical group that has taken the world by storm, one that has fired the passions of teen fans more than Duran Duran, the Bay City Rollers, and Menudo all put together, and to be the first act since the Beatles to have the top two entries on the Hot 100 in the same month, and the first group *ever* to have a number one album and single on the charts at the same time? In short, what's it like to be a superstar?

It's hard work, that's what!

The New Kids On The Block have been called "the hardest working kids in show business," and it's the truth! Through all this, Joe has only one regret. He doesn't have as much time to spend at home with his family. Lately, he has been moving in perpetual motion and living a very hectic life on the road. But this happy kid wouldn't trade in his success for anything!

Joe is quick to list all the things he can't do while on tour. "I never have time to just sit back and flick on a TV," he says. "And, of course, I like playing basketball, football, and baseball. But when we're traveling, we usually go from the bus to the hotel room to the stage."

Traveling, rehearsing, polishing their dance routines, learning new songs, and performing in different cities all over the world may sound glamorous, but it's more hard work than anything else.

Despite the hard work, Joe is having a great time

performing with the group. "We're like brothers," he says of his friendships with Donnie, Jordan, Jon, and Danny. "And I think that's why we're so popular with teens. They can tell by our chemistry onstage that we're having a good time. So they have a good time, too."

The one thing Joe misses most when he's out on tour is his own bedroom. "I really look forward to coming home and staying in my own bed."

Success has taken away his privacy, too. In fact, none of the kids have much of a private life anymore. The most time they have alone is at night in a hotel room. Even then some fans manage to find out their room numbers and telephone them all through the night.

In spite of all that, Joe and the others love what they do, and they love their fans! There's something about walking onstage every night in front of 20,000 screaming fans and performing for them that makes it all worthwhile.

One of the reasons New Kids mania has swept the nation is because they have a message to convey. Take the song, "Hangin' Tough," for example. The song seems to say, "just be yourself and hang tough." Teens have responded to that, and it's one of the reasons the group has become so popular.

Joe explains another reason why they've taken off as they have, "There just weren't any groups like us! Young black kids could look up to New Edition, and there was Menudo. But there wasn't a young white group that could be a good role model for teens. We've been very lucky that we were given the chance. If there are a million people in the music business, there are two million waiting to get in."

One of the things Joe likes to do when he finally gets home is catch up on his reading. His favorite books are mysteries. Another way he relaxes is when he indulges

Traveling is great, but Joe misses his mom's meatloaf and sleeping in his own bed. Mike Gustella, Star File

in his favorite hobby—playing golf. "I love the game," he says. "It's really very relaxing, but challenging at the same time."

Then it's back on the road again. It's no secret that fame has a high price, but the Kids aren't complaining. In the past few years, Joe and the others have traveled from the smallest towns to the largest cities in the United States and to faraway places like Japan, Hawaii, and European capitals.

Like anything else, there are good and bad aspects about being superstars and traveling so much. One of the good things is that Joe gets to meet a lot of new people and make new friends in every city he travels through.

Recently, Joe and the others got beepers to wear when they're on the road so they can be contacted by their parents at any time. When the beeper sounds, it

"Being onstage with the New Kids is the best time of my life," says Joe. "We have so much fun." Ernie Paniccioli

means it's time to call home and find out what's going on with the family. Somehow, knowing that their families are just a beep away gives them a real sense of security. "If there's an emergency, it's easier for our folks to let us know," says Joe. "I talk to my folks all the time!"

The New Kids travel in a tour bus to get from one city to the next. Life gets hectic living on the road, and it's tough sleeping on a bus. So they try to do everything they can to make their grueling schedule fun.

Sleeping on the bus may be difficult, but at least they each have their own bed. In fact, the bus has been set up to be their "home away from home." In the back of the bus they have an area called the "living room," complete with a well-stocked refrigerator, a TV set, stereo, VCR, and plenty of video games (lots of Nintendo) and movies.

Actually, three buses in all are needed to carry the backup band, stage crew, equipment, and bodyguards. Though Joe usually travels in the same bus with Donnie and Danny, and Jon and Jordan share another bus, it isn't unusual to see the New Kids riding with the crew.

After a show, Joe and the others usually have a ten to twelve hour drive to the next town. What do they do to pass the time? "Sleep, mostly," says Joe. And no wonder, because by the time they finish a concert, pack up, and head out of town, it's sometimes as late as 3:00 a.m.!

A lot of their time is spent in hotels, too. This calls for heavy security precautions on the part of the hotel's management. It isn't that the New Kids don't want to mingle with their fans, it's just that if word got out which floor they were on, there'd be a riot! And nobody wants that.

So when Joe and the others check into a hotel (reservations are made far in advance), they are given an entire floor! Each New Kid has his own room, and guards are placed at all entrances and exits, so their privacy is assured. In spite of all that, some overzealous fans still try to sneak in.

The New Kids aren't exactly the neatest guys in the world when it comes to their hotel rooms—reporters have observed clothes and crumpled socks lying around on the floor. That's not too bad, when you consider what some rock groups do to hotel rooms. The New Kids respect other people's property and never damage anything. They may wrestle and have pillow fights to let off steam, but that's about it.

What does Joe do when he's alone in his hotel room? Sleep, watch TV, and the most fun of all—order room service! What does he usually order? A hamburger or hotdog, fries, potato salad, and chips. It's a typical teen menu because Joe's a typical teenager!

Meanwhile, back on the bus, what do the Kids do to pass the time when they're not sleeping? Talk mostly. They sit around in a circle and just rap together. Sometimes, Joe and the others will have a "brainstorming" session. This is where they get new ideas for their act, and sometimes come up with new songs!

It's also a good time to open up all the gifts and stuff fans send them or toss up onstage. They appreciate the gesture and enjoy the pleasure of opening gifts, but they rarely keep anything. Instead, they donate most of it to children's hospitals or homes for the needy in the cities they visit.

What is a typical day for Joe and the others like when they hit a town for a concert? They usually arrive early in the morning, having traveled all night. Then it's time to check into the hotel, freshen up, eat breakfast, and rehearse from eleven in the morning until around two in the afternoon. At about four in the afternoon, they have to go to the concert hall, arena, or stadium to do a "sound check," so their fans won't

oe with his friend Dino, a former Las Vegas deejay who toured with he New Kids last winter. Janet Macoska

niss hearing a single note or word they say.

Then there are always interviews with the local ress, radio, and TV people. This is very important, nd they might wind up meeting the mayor of the own, the governor, and other important people.

By now, it's after five o'clock, and time to start hinking about having dinner. After they eat, they have o begin getting ready for the show! Their concerts usually begin around 8:00 p.m. and end around 11:00 .m.

They have to arrive at the venue about an hour be-ore they go on. This gives them time to get dressed they change clothes several times during each per-ormance), and drink a special blend of honey and emon tea. This not only soothes their throats, but the oney gives them the much needed boost of energy hey'll use up in the time they are onstage.

After spending some time fixing their hair (using ots of hairspray), it's time to get psyched for the show. ince they are almost always excited, it doesn't take much to get them going. There is one ritual they always do, which is to get into a huddle like football players, just the five of them. What they say in that huddle is strictly between them. Whatever they say sure works, because when they come out of it, they are ready to hit that stage and take it by storm!

The Kids are in a frenzy out there, prancing, dancing, stepping high, breakdancing, all the while singing, and occasionally reaching out to touch the hands of lucky fans seated down front.

Anyone who has ever seen a New Kids On The Block concert will tell you they really put on a show. The total effect of their carefully staged dance routines, spotlights, lasers, and superb sound system and backup band is overwhelming. The New Kids really move! They fill the stage and seem larger than life!

When Joe does his solos, the crowd goes wild. Nothing in the world beats thousands of fans screaming their approval of what you do. For Joe, it's the ultimate.

Sometimes, Joe or one of the others will invite a fan up onstage and sing a song especially to her. It just shows how the New Kids really feel about their fans. They enjoy getting close to them, and actually talking to them if they can.

In the beginning, the Kids had pre-recorded music backing them. That was quickly replaced by a live backup band. Then they quietly and diligently began learning how to play instruments. Now they give their fans an extra treat when they suddenly pick up instruments and begin playing and singing! It makes for a great jam session, and the crowds love it!

After the show, the New Kids are always swarmed by fans. They've even had jackets ripped right off their backs and torn into shreds, so their bodyguards try to keep them away from the crowds for security reasons.

So, what's it like to be superstars? As you can see, it

volves a lot of hard work, grueling travel, loneliness, nd homesickness. But in the end, it's worth it, not nly for the great financial rewards, but for the smiles nd joy that Joe and the other Kids see on the faces of heir fans. That's what it's really all about!

n and Joe—the oldest and youngest of the New Kids. Star File

BEING A ROLE MODEL

A lot comes with success. Fame, fortune, being idolized by millions of fans, but most of all, with success comes responsibility. A responsibility to be at your best at all times, to give your best performance, no matter how you feel or what your mental or physical state is. Riding on top of all that is also the responsibility of being a good role model for all those who look up to you.

A lot or rock groups are slack in that department. Their behavior is nothing to be admired, and certainly, nothing to be emulated. That's what separates Joe and the other New Kids from other groups. They have more going for them than just a good performance— they have character.

Put simply, Joe and the other Kids are nice people. That quality comes across onstage, so the fans respond to it, and know that they're real people. Their being nice isn't just an act. It's really the way they are!

Joe comes from a very religious family and his parents were concerned when he first joined New Kids. They'd heard about members of other rock groups who'd gotten involved in drugs and alcohol; often with fatal results. They certainly did not want that for their little Joe. So before she let him go, Joe's mom had a nice long talk with him. She knew it wouldn't be easy for Joe out there on the road, staying in hotels, sleeping overnight on buses, and trying to keep a level head while thousands of girls across America screamed their adoration at him night after night.

Joe's mom wanted to make sure that he attended Mass each week while he was on the road, and reminded him that his voice was a gift. So no matter what city he's in, Joe tries to observe his religious prac-

e, Danny, Jon, Donnie, and Jordan (left to right) enjoying New rk's Central Park. Ernie Paniccioli

es. He does it quietly and privately and doesn't ake a big deal about it.

Though it's tough to balance a spiritual life with a ow business life, a lot of performers do it. Joe and e other New Kids are trying to hold on to that, be- use they know how valuable it is to them.

The fact that so many fans look up to them has made e and the others realize how important it is for them be good role models. Popularity has given them the wer to speak to a lot of kids, to reach them on their wn terms. So they immediately got involved with the ust Say No To Drugs'' campaign, and they have orked many long hours for that organization.

While growing up, all the New Kids were pressured

to try drugs. Fortunately, they would have no part of it. Joe has been saying "No" to drugs all his life, long before it became a national slogan.

Joe and the others make a lot of trips to high schools just to speak to students about the dangers of drugs. Not only will they appear at a high school, they will actually go into the classroom and talk to the students about saying "No" to drugs. Then they might perform a couple of songs before leaving.

Another point the New Kids try to make is for students to stay in school. Staying in school and saying "No" to drugs are just about the two most important issues facing America's kids today. The New Kids feel it's important to reach these kids, because they are peers as well as fans!

Joe and the others accompanied Massachusetts Governor Michael Dukakis on his statewide campaign against drugs and performed at various anti-drug rallies, including the Governor's Alliance Against Drugs. They even recorded a rap song with Boston Mayor Raymond L. Flynn which told kids to "just be yourself and don't be doin' drugs!"

Another important cause the guys support and donate their services to is United Cerebral Palsy. They've appeared for three years in a row on the nationally televised United Cerebral Palsy Telethon, and helped raise so much money for this cause that they have been named UCP teen spokesmen.

They also took part in the Annual Bike-A-Thon for UCP in Manhattan's Central Park. Besides raising more than $750,000 for UCP, the Kids hung out with their fans, signed autographs, and posed for just about anybody who had a camera. The fans went away knowing that the New Kids were nice, caring people.

Joe and the others never got together and said they were going to be good role models. It's not a part of a plan, or some kind of image they want to build. It

oe's advice—be yourself and believe in yourself. Janet Macoska

Too little sleep while touring takes its toll on Joe. Todd Kaplan, Star File

imply the way they are. And the one thing Joe and the others insist upon is being themselves!

The New Kids say if you're on the streets, you're asking for trouble. Instead, play sports, play music, find a hobby. Just get off the streets, because there isn't anything there for you. If some sucker offers you drugs, just say, "NO!" You'll be glad you did. Joe McIntyre often appears onstage in concert wearing a T-shirt that says: DRUG FREE BODY. That's how serious he is about it!

If Joe and the others have an overall message to their fans, it's simply this: Learn how to feel good about yourself. Everything springs from that. You can't help others or even love others until you feel good about yourself.

The New Kids encourage individualism. You'll notice they don't dress alike, as a lot of other groups do. Each New Kid dresses in his own particular style. It's his way of expressing himself and of making his own personal statement. They know that being an individual is the best thing to be. That way you don't have to give in to peer pressure. You can say, "Hey, man, I'm me! You're you! What's okay for you is fine, but it's not for me!" In other words, do what your heart tells you to do.

Joe sums it up with, "It's not what's out there in the world that you have to worry about. It's what's in your heart and in your head."

THE FUTURE

What's around the block for this New Kid On The Block? Joe's present looks bright, no question about that. The second album, *Hangin' Tough,* has sold more than ten million copies and from that came four top ten singles. Their latest album, *Step By Step,* is already double platinum. Thousands of fan letters come in every week to the New Kids Fan Club, and over 100,000 phone calls a week are made to the New Kids' 900 number.

Wherever they appear in concert, their performances are sold out long before they even hit town. Joe and the other New Kids truly have reached the top of their profession.

Even adults attend their shows. "They make me feel like a teenager," said one mom who came with her daughter and stood in line for hours before the show.

Joe admits he simply wasn't ready for such mad adoration. Every day it seems to get crazier and crazier. Fans have popped up out of hotel garbage cans just to get a close look at them as they passed by, sprawled down in front of their limos, even taken lawn trimmings from the front of the Kids' homes, and tried disguising themselves as maids to get into their hotel rooms.

Joe knows that the best way to handle it is to have fun with it, and have a few laughs. As far as the New Kids go, Joe says, "We just see each other as regular

The ultimate role models—NKOTB all say "NO" to drugs!
odd Kaplan, Star File

ids." Of course, their fans don't see it that way. To
hem the New Kids On The Block are special. Very
pecial.

Their new album, *Step By Step,* is a blockbuster fol-
owup to their last, *Hangin' Tough,* and *Merry, Merry*

Christmas had quadruple platinum sales. Every tune in *Step By Step* is an original song. It was recorded while they were on the road, with each New Kid getting solos. They also co-wrote many of the songs. Their fans are already looking forward to album number five!

Their 60-concert North American tour which began June 23 is sold out. The inside story is that it's a radical all-new show with lots of high-tech special effects and some new choreographed dance routines that really sizzle!

They're playing large stadiums this time out, instead of concert halls in cities all over the country. Some of these stadiums hold 60,000 fans and more!

What happens after the tour? Work on the movie will be beginning and though there's no title for it as yet, it could be released next summer.

What kind of movie is it going to be? A comedy, more than likely. Every time something funny happens to the New Kids, whether on tour or at a recording studio, one of them will invariably yell out, "Hey, let's put that in the movie!" So they've been putting their ideas on tape to save them.

Naturally, they had their choice of producer and were able to pick and choose. They finally settled on the production team mostly likely to assure them of a hit—none other than Peter Guber and Jon Peters of Columbia Pictures who gave the world the megablockbuster, *Batman!*

How about the New Kids as a Saturday morning cartoon show? You bet! Television looms big in the Kids' future. An animated early morning Saturday cartoon series based on them will begin this fall on ABC. The show will open with a live-action, fast-paced montage of one of their songs and end with them in performance. It will feature action-adventure stories starring the Kids.

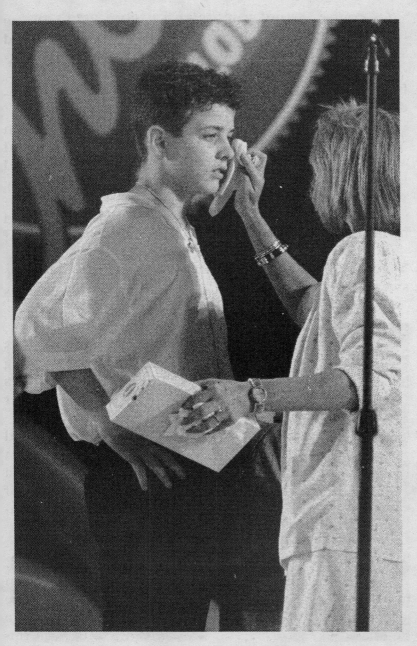

Joe gets some help preparing for a television taping. Janet Macoska

Of course, Saturday morning cartoons aren't the only place you can expect the New Kids to pop up on TV. They've already shown up on various award shows, and there's talk of Disney presenting them in a full-length video. Even as you read this there are more deals in the works, and you can bet there'll be no shortage of New Kids' products.

If Michael Jackson can have a doll made in his image, why not Joe McIntyre and the other New Kids? Hasbro has just put out a line of New Kids dolls, which will come with their own onstage and offstage costumes. There is also a stage set, complete with bandstand, microphones, and musical instruments.

A full line of New Kids clothes are also available. You'll find New Kids denim jackets, oversized T-shirts, sweat shirts, hats, and even buttons to wear.

Joe is aware that when a group gets this popular,

Superstar Joe still enjoys life's simple pleasures—his family, old friends, and a game of basketball. Steve Granitz/Retna

there's always gossip that one or two of them might break away from the group and go solo. It's a danger all groups face. The possibility of them breaking up looms darkly in the background. It happened to the Beatles, the Jackson Five, and a lot of others.

Could that happen to the New Kids? Most likely, it won't. It's all still so new to them. They have too much going for them now. The freshness is still there. That, coupled with the fact that in the past few years they have become like brothers. "Onstage is the best time of our lives," says Joe. "We have so much fun!"

It is a team effort. That's why Joe and the others work so well together. Occasionally, they'll have a disagreement, but that's normal, and they get over it very fast.

The truth is Joe and the others would like to see the group enjoy years and years of success. To do that, they have to stay together. As for long-term future aspirations, they all have their separate dreams.

Mostly, they want to have families and live normal, regular lives. Some of them want to work in the music business, behind the scenes, as writers, producers, and recording executives. Joe McIntyre leans more in that direction. Says Joe, "I'd like to learn more behind the scenes stuff about the music biz, and learn to become a producer like Maurice Starr. Who knows? Maybe one day, I'll even start a group like New Kids On The Block!"

Joe is working hard at becoming a better musician. It's true that when he joined the group, they didn't have to play musical instruments. But Joe is bent on improving himself. So are the rest of the New Kids. Joe is studying both the piano and the guitar! So when the concert tour comes to your town, you'll see the New Kids pick up instruments and play them quite well.

What Joe and the others want to do is please everybody. Of course, no one can do that, but they try, boy, do they try! Take autographs, for example. It's tough to be able to give every fan who asks an autograph. It's impossible, that's what! So a lot of fans go away disappointed. "We really try to please everyone," says Joe. "But when hundreds of kids rush up to us wanting autographs, we don't always have the time." If it's any consolation, remember, it hurts the New Kids just as much as it hurts their fans.

Looking into the future can present a lot of problems, especially if you look too far into the future! Their name, for example—how long can they go on being called New Kids On The Block? Five years from now they won't be so new anymore. "Young Men On The Block" sounds really weird!

Joe and the others have talked to their producer about that problem. They've been told that as time passes their name will change. Into what is anybody's guess, but for now, the plan is to stay exactly the way they are!

Whatever the future holds for Joe and the others, they will continue spreading their message for drug-free bodies, clean air, homes for the homeless, and a positive self-image.

MORE ABOUT JOE

Joe McIntyre is the kind of guy any girl could really flip out over. He's sweet and so innocent looking, girls just want to hug him. He's very friendly and will talk to anybody. The reason? Joe sincerely likes people! Being the youngest of nine children, Joe had better like people—he's been surrounded by them all his life!

Joe has a great sense of humor. He developed it through years of joking and kidding around with his brother and sisters. He's chilled out. Fun. Sensitive but not overly sentimental. And, of course, he's a family man. Just the kind of guy who would make a good husband and father.

Joe and Danny enjoying a good laugh. Chris Mackie

Joe enjoys reading, especially mysteries, but that doesn't mean that he prefers to be off by himself, either. He's a very balanced sort of fellow, and likes to have time alone, as well as time to join the crowd and go with the flow. He loves a good discussion (some people might call them arguments) because he has very definite opinions which he doesn't hesitate to voice.

Joe has led a more sheltered life than the other New Kids, but he's learned a lot since hooking up with the group. All this traveling around the world, meeting new people, and tasting super-stardom has had its effect upon him. So while he looks like an innocent kid—he's been around a bit! He describes himself as "funny, somewhat of a wise guy, worried, and chilled."

More than anything else, Joe is determined to have a successful musical career, but, according to him, his most important goal in life is to have peace of mind. Underneath all the hype and glamour, Joe is basically a very serious guy. He is concerned with problems in the world, such as drugs, war, and poverty. He'd like to help the homeless, which makes sense, because home is very important to him.

We know Joe is committed to his career, but what about girls? Does he have a steady girlfriend? The answer at this stage of the game is, no! Being a superstar and on the road all the time really gets in the way of that! There simply isn't time to develop a lasting relationship.

Joe says, "I'm not really looking for a girlfriend right now. But if a girl catches my eye, I'll talk to her. I'd like to meet someone who is independent and who has her own personality. Someone cool, chill and smart."

And where would he take his dream girl? "To Disneyland," dreams Joe. "Without a doubt. It's the ulti-

Fans at a NKOTB concert are really treated to a terrific show, and when Joe does his solo, the crowd goes wild! Ernie Paniccioli

mate. With all those rides and exhibits, you can't miss having a good time!''

Joe prefers girls who have interests and goals of their own, who have things going for themselves. He'll talk about anything in the world—movies, music, TV, sports, whatever. So, there's never any lull in the conversation when you're around Joe.

Pushy girls make him uncomfortable. A real turnoff are girls who rush up to him and say, "I love you!" without even knowing him. He also hates liars and people who are deceitful in any way. But his biggest turnoff is when someone hangs out just to be "seen" with him. He wants to be liked for the person he is, not for the fact that he's part of New Kids On The Block.

Joe has been described as "the major heartthrob of the group." However, he doesn't see himself (or any member of the group) that way. Says Joe, "We're not those big perfect, awesome dudes who can do any-

Joe still idolizes Michael Jackson, but his current favorite is Frank Sinatra. Chris Mackie

thing, and I hope our fans don't think we are. We're like our fans—in fact, we're just like them!''

Joe doesn't even think he's much to look at! "Girls say I'm cute," he says bashfully. But he dismisses it with, "I don't think I'm cute. It must be my big feet!"

"I like girls," he laughs, "but I don't think of myself as a heartbreaker. I'm a big flirt, but it's innocent!"

He did have a crush on a girl when he was twelve years old. It was just before he joined New Kids. "We were both in the Neighborhood Children's Theater," he recalls, "and because all my friends were flirting with girls, we sort of liked each other for six months or so. The first time she broke it off, and I cried. Then the second time, I broke it off."

Joe thinks it would be nice if he met a girl who didn't know too much about New Kids On The Block, one who just happened to come to the concert and liked what she saw, and thought they put on a good show.

One thing most people don't know about Joe is that he's quite the impressionist. He can do impressions of each New Kid and he's got them down so well, it really cracks them up. Joe got his start doing impressions early in life imitating members of his family.

One of Joe's worst qualities is that he is definitely not a good loser, but he gets over it pretty fast.

On the positive side, Joe is very generous and thoughtful. When Joe was unable to attend his sister Judith's appearance in *Peg Of My Heart* on Broadway, he sent a dozen roses to her at the theater along with a card wishing her good luck.

What are Joe's likes and dislikes? His favorite food is meatloaf—his mom's, of course! His first favorite singer was Elton John. Right now, his favorite is (would you believe?) Frank Sinatra! If you were to go out on a date with him, he'd probably slap a cassette of old Frank on the stereo. Joe also loves ice cream sun-

49

daes, and likes to make them himself!

How does Joe like to dress? It's simple, really. Joe doesn't dress any differently than any other normal, wholesome American teenager. He usually wears just a plain button-down shirt or T-shirt with jeans. But since he loves cartoon characters, he might liven things up by wearing a Mickey Mouse or a Felix The Cat jacket.

What are some of the words Joe uses a lot? Well, "chill" or "chillin'" show up a lot in his conversation.

Sweet Sensation (left to right: Betty D., Sheila, Margie) are just one of many groups who have opened for the New Kids. Robin Platzer

They simply mean staying loose, hanging back, or just plain relaxing.

Another favorite word is "dis." It's short for disrespectful. So when you "dis" someone, you've said something negative about that person.

"Dude," of course, is a guy or a friend.

"Homeboy" is a friend from the neighborhood.

"Go ill" is to be cool.

"Posse" is a backup band or a group of friends.

What is the best part of being with New Kids On The Block? Joe says, "I like the concerts best, because I think you get the full effect of all our hard work. It's the time to get the feedback from the audience and see how you really are doing with them and the music."

Joe's most embarrassing moment came a couple of years ago, when the New Kids were opening for Tiffany. "Tiff was watching from the wings when she suddenly started cracking up. My pants had split open!" Joe laughs. "Another time, some fans were throwing stuff up on the stage, and I got hit in the face with a stuffed animal!"

Joe is probably considered the most friendly of the New Kids (although they are all very friendly) because he is always the first one out of the dressing room to meet fans backstage after a concert.

Joe also loves to hang out at the mall. Any mall in any city. Trouble with that is, now he gets recognized, so it can be a problem. He could probably get away with wearing a disguise, but that's a drag to do, and it's still no guarantee that he won't be recognized.

Right now, Joe's life revolves around the New Kids and his family. He also likes to write, and he toys with the idea of someday becoming a journalist or even writing a book. Rumor has it that he's keeping a diary. If that's so, then a book about his experiences with New Kids On The Block would be something to look forward to!

Vinnie Zuffante, Star File

Jordan and Joe—two of the sweetest singing voices you've ever heard! Janet Macoska

Who knows what the future holds for Joe McIntyre? Joe certainly plans on marriage sometime in the future. He's still got a lot of living to do first. However, he is definitely looking! One thing is for sure, Joe and the other New Kids will continue making music, recording, and performing for as long as their fans want them to, and the way things are going now, that could be for a long, long time!

JUST THE FACTS

Full Name: Joseph Mulrey McIntyre
Nicknames: Joe Bird, Joey Joe, Bird
Birthdate: December 31, 1972
Birthplace: Needham, Massachusetts
Hair: Blondish brown
Eyes: Blue
Height: 5′ 6″
Weight: 120 lbs.
Shoe Size: 8 1/2
Shirt Size: Small
Parents: Thomas and Kay
Brother & Sisters: Judith, Alice, Susan, Patricia, Carol, Jean, Kate, Tom
Favorite Actors: Bill Cosby, Robert DeNiro
Favorite Actress: His sister, Judith
Favorite Movies: *Big, Beverly Hills Cop, Midnight Run*
Favorite TV Shows: *Cheers, Monday Night Football*
Favorite Bands: Huey Lewis and the News, The Temptations
Favorite Food: Mexican
Favorite Drink: Classic Coke
Favorite Clothes: ''Anything comfortable!''
Favorite Car: BMW 325 with phone
Favorite Colors: Blue, red
Favorite Sports: Golf, basketball, bowling
Favorite Childhood Memory: ''Christmas with my family''
Biggest Influence: His family
Musical Instruments: Studying the piano and the guitar
Main Goals: ''To have peace of mind.''
Ideal Girl: ''Cool, chill, smart, independent, and

charming. Must have good sense of humor.''

Ideal Date: Go to a movie and dinner or to Disneyland

Self-Description: ''Funny, peaceful, worried, and chill.''

Best Quality: ''I'm smart.''

Worst Quality: ''I can't stand losing.''

Most Prized Possession: His family

PART 4

MUSIC AND VIDEOS

New Kids On The Block (Columbia, April 1986; Re-released 1989)
Tracks: "Stop It Girl" (M. Starr); "Didn't I (Blow Your Mind)?" (W. Hart, T. Bell); "Popsicle" (M. Starr); "Angel" (M. Starr, J. Cappra); "Be My Girl" (M. Starr); "New Kids On The Block" (M. Starr, D. Wahlberg); "Are You Down?" (AJ, E. Nuri, K. Banks, D. Wahlberg); "I Wanna Be Loved By You" (M. Starr); "Don't Give Up On Me" (M. Starr); "Treat Me Right" (M. Starr).

Hangin' Tough (Columbia, March 1988)
Tracks: "You Got It (The Right Stuff)" (M. Starr); "Please Don't Go Girl" (M. Starr); "I Need You" (M. Starr); "I'll Be Loving You (Forever)" (M. Starr); "Cover Girl" (M. Starr); "I Need You" (M. Starr); "Hangin' Tough" (M. Starr); "I Remember When" (M. Starr, E. Kelly, J. Randolph, C. Williams); "What'cha Gonna Do (About It)" (M. Starr); "My Favorite Girl" (M. Starr, D. Wahlberg, J. Knight); "Hold On" (M. Starr).

Merry, Merry Christmas (Columbia, September 1989)
Tracks: "This One's For The Children" (M. Starr); "Last Night I Saw Santa Claus" (M. Starr, A. Lancellotti); "I'll Be Missin' You Come Christmas (A Letter To Santa)" (K. Nolan, M. Starr); "I Still Believe In Santa Claus" (M. Starr, A. Lancellotti); "Merry, Merry Christmas" (M. Starr, A. Lancellotti); "The Christmas Song (Chestnuts Roasting On An Open Fire)" (M. Torme, R. Wells); "Funky, Funky Xmas" (M. Starr, D. Wahlberg); "White Christmas" (I. Berlin); "Little Drummer Boy" (K.K. Davis, B. Onorati, H. Simeone, adaptation by J. Edwards); "This One's For The Children" (Reprise).

Step By Step (Columbia, June 1990)
Tracks: Side One: "Step By Step" (M. Starr); "Tonight" (M. Starr, A. Lancellotti); "Baby, I Believe In You" (M. Starr); "Call It What You Want" (M. Starr); "Let's Try It Again" (M. Starr); "Happy Birthday" (M. Starr, M. Jonzun).

Side Two: "Games" (M. Starr, D. Wahlberg); "Time Is On Our Side" (M. Starr, A. Lancellotti); "Where Do We Go From Here?" (M. Starr); "Stay With Me, Baby" (M. Starr, M. Jonzun); "Funny Feeling" (M. Starr, M. Jonzun); "Never Gonna Fall In Love Again" (M. Starr, M. Jonzun, D. Wood).

Singles: "Step By Step" released 5/90; future singles not announced at press time.

SINGLES
"Be My Girl"
"Stop It Girl"
"Didn't I (Blow Your Mind)?"
"Please Don't Go Girl"
"You Got It (The Right Stuff)"
"I'll Be Loving You (Forever)"
"Cover Girl"
"Hangin' Tough"
"This One's For The Children"
"Step By Step"

MUSIC VIDEOS
"Please Don't Go Girl"
"You Got It (The Right Stuff)"
"I'll Be Loving You (Forever)"
"Cover Girl"
"Didn't I (Blow Your Mind)?"
"Hangin' Tough"
"This One's For The Children"
"Step By Step"

VIDEOCASSETTES
HANGIN' TOUGH (CBS Home Video, 1989)
This 30-minute home video contains interviews and backstage footage as well as videos for the four hits off the *Hangin' Tough* LP: "Please Don't Go Girl," "You Got It (The Right Stuff)," "I'll Be Loving You (Forever)" and "Hangin' Tough."

HANGIN' TOUGH LIVE (CBS Home Video, 1989)
Every New Kids hit off their second LP is performed live in this half-hour-long cassette.

AWARDS AND HONORS

AMERICAN MUSIC AWARDS
—Favorite Pop/Rock Album (*Hangin' Tough*)
—Favorite Pop/Rock Group

BOSTON MUSIC AWARDS
—Outstanding Pop/Rock Single ("I'll Be Loving You Forever")
—Outstanding Video ("Hangin' Tough")
—Act Of The Year

GRAMMY NOMINATION
—Best Music Video (Long Form)

ON TOUR

European and Magic Summer Tour Photos

Meyer/Fotex/Shooting Star

NEW KIDS ON THE BLOCK
Five More Sensational Books About Those Five Fabulous Guys!

Packed with facts and filled with wonderful black and white photos.

10515
10525
10545
10540

10510

Each digest-size (5 ¼″ × 8 ¼″) 64-page book is only $2.50 plus an additional .50 for postage/handling for each book. (No COD's).

This large-format (8 ¼″ × 10 ¾″) 64-page scrapbook (with spaces to paste in your own favorite photos) is only $3.00 plus an additional $1.00 for postage/handling for each book. (No COD's).